Mark Ravenhill

Ten Plagues

a libretto

and

The Coronation of Poppea

freely ~~*d*~~ *from the libretto by Giovanni Francesco Busenello*
f ~~~~ *oronazione di Poppea by Claudio Monteverdi*

Published by Methuen Drama 2011

Methuen Drama, an imprint of Bloomsbury Publishing Plc

1 3 5 7 9 10 8 6 4 2

Methuen Drama
Bloomsbury Publishing Plc
36 Soho Square
London W1D 3QY
www.methuendrama.com

ISBN 978 1 408 16054 1

A CIP catalogue record for this book is
available from the British Library

Available in the USA from Bloomsbury Academic & Professional,
175 Fifth Avenue/3rd Floor, New York, NY 10010.
www.BloomsburyAcademicUSA.com

Typeset by Mark Heslington Ltd, Scarborough, North Yorkshire
Printed and bound in Great Britain by CPI Cox & Wyman, Reading,
RG1 8EX

TRAVERSE
THEATRE

Traverse Theatre Company
Produced in association with David Johnson

Ten Plagues

By Mark Ravenhill and Conor Mitchell

Libretto by Mark Ravenhill
Music by Conor Mitchell
Directed and Designed by Stewart Laing
Performed by Marc Almond

Musical Director Bob Broad
Assistant Director David Betz-Heinemann
Movement Director Theo Clinkard
Lighting Designer Zerlina Hughes
Video Designer Finn Ross

Video Performer Francis Christeller.

Stage Manager Dan Dixon
Deputy Stage Manager Rachel Gillard
Technician Fraiser Thomson Noble

Costumer Supervisor John Liddell
Wig Consultant Campbell Young
Costume made by Scottish Open Costume Department

First performed at the Traverse Theatre,
Monday 1 August 2011.

Traverse Theatre
Artistic Director Dominic Hill

"The Traverse has an unrivalled reputation for producing contemporary theatre of the highest quality, invention and energy, and for its dedication to new writing."
Scotland on Sunday

The Traverse Theatre is Scotland's new writing theatre. From its conception in 1963, it has embraced a spirit of innovation and risk taking that launched the careers of many of Scotland's best-known writers including John Byrne, David Greig, David Harrower and Liz Lochhead. It is unique in Scotland in that it fulfils the crucial role of providing the infrastructure, professional support and expertise to ensure the development of a dynamic theatre culture for Scotland. It commissions and develops new plays or adaptations from contemporary playwrights. It produces, on average, six Traverse Theatre Company productions or co-productions per year. It also presents a large number of productions from visiting companies from across the UK. These include new plays, adaptations, dance, physical theatre, puppetry and contemporary music.

The Traverse is a pivotal venue in Edinburgh and this is particularly the case during the Edinburgh Festival in August – positioned as it is between the Edinburgh Festival Fringe and the Edinburgh International Festival.

The Traverse is also the home of the Manipulate Visual Theatre Festival, the Bank of Scotland Imaginate Festival and the Traverse's own Autumn Festival.

"A Rolls-Royce machine for promoting new Scottish drama across Europe and beyond."
The Scotsman

The Traverse's work with young people is of major importance and takes the form of encouraging playwriting through its flagship education project Class Act, as well as the Young Writers' Group. Class Act recently celebrated its twenty-first anniversary and has given school pupils the opportunity to develop their plays with professional playwrights and work with directors and actors to see the finished piece performed on stage at the Traverse. The hugely successful Young Writers' Group is open to new writers aged 18 – 25. Scribble offers an after-school playwriting and theatre skills workshop for 14 – 17 year olds. Both programmes are led by professional playwrights.

Traverse Theatre (Scotland) Limited, registered in Scotland SC 076037. Registered Charity No. SC 002368, VAT reg. no. 356 0682 47. Registered Office: Traverse Theatre, Cambridge Street, Edinburgh, EH1 2ED

Company Biographies

Marc Almond

Marc Almond is an internationally successful artist who has worked in many musical styles and has sold over thirty million records worldwide. Marc spent five years studying Fine Art and Performance at Leeds Polytechnic before forming the record-breaking band Soft Cell with Dave Ball. In 1982, Marc began to experiment with Flamenco, Turkish Torch Songs and 'twisted Cabaret Pop'. Since Soft Cell's split in 1984, Marc has pursued an eventful and diverse solo-career in both the mainstream and underground, producing over twelve albums. Over the years Marc has collaborated with diverse artists including Nick Cave, Siouxsie, John Cale, Nico, Antony Hegarty, Gene Pitney Baby Dee, Bronski Beat, PJ Proby and Jools Holland. As well as a large body of recorded work, he has also released two best-selling autobiographies, *Tainted Life* and *In Search of the Pleasure Palace*, as well as collections of poems and verse. In 2009 he released a collection of Russian folk songs, *Orpheus in Exile*, the songs of Vadim Kozin and in 2010 he celebrated thirty years in music with a new album *Variete*. Marc's new album *Feasting With Panthers*, a collaboration with Berlin based musician Michael Cashmore, was released earlier this year.

David Betz-Heinemann (Assistant Director)

David trained on the MFA Theatre Directing course at Birkbeck College, London. Directing work for the Traverse includes: *Four Parts Broken* (National Theatre of Scotland/Òran Mór); *Class Act 21* and as assistant director on *Pandas, Welcome to the Hotel Caledonia, The Three Musketeers and the Princess of Spain* (in co-production with English Touring Theatre and the Belgrade Theatre, Coventry) and *Impossible Things Before Breakfast*. Other work assisting includes: *Tom's Midnight Garden* (Nottingham Playhouse); *The Pride* (Sheffield Crucible); *The Big Script* (Soho Theatre) and *Figaro Gets Divorced* (Cochrane). David has also directed new work for Kids Company (National Theatre Studio); the London Arts Orchestra and Old Vic New Voice. David is Artistic Director of *People at Play* at Pimilco Academy, London.

Bob Broad (Musical Director)

Bob studied at both Trinity College of Music and the Royal Academy of Music, gaining hisBMus(Hons)TCM and PGDip from Trinity, in Organ and Piano Accompaniment, and PGDipRam in Musical Theatre Direction/ Coaching from the Academy. Recordings and broadcasts include BBC Radio 3 and 4, and on the Opera Omnia label for Cancer Research. In

2003 he was awarded the FASC (Academy of Saint Cecilia); in 2005 he won the London Cardnell Organ prize, and in 2006 won 1st prize at the International Handel Festival for Accompaniment. More recently Bob received the Cameron Macintosh Prize for Accompaniment in Song (2008). Musical Directing work includes: *Betty Blue Eyes* (Novello Theatre); *Cradle Will Rock* (Arcola Theatre, London); *Silence, The Musical* (Stag Theatre, London); *Jest-End* (Jermyn Street Theatre, London); *A Slice Of Saturday Night* (Edinburgh Festival); *A Night At The Theatre* (Manchester Royal Exchange/ Soho Theatre). As a rehearsal pianist: *Tick Tick..... Boom* (Duchess Theatre, London); *The Last Five Years* (Duchess Theatre, London); *A Man Of No Importance* (Arts Theatre, London). Keyboards: *They're Playing Our Song* (Menier Chocolate Factory) *High School Musical* (UK Tour) *Witches Of Eastwick* (UK Tour). He worked as Vocal Coach on *The Beat Goes On* (Channel 5, Gallowgate Productions) and repititeur for *A Dogs Heart* (Complicite/English National Opera).

Bob also currently works in London's West-End as an Audition Pianist (for Casting Agents, West-End productions, Commercial Agencies, Corporate recordings and Personal Management), Rehearsal Pianist, Repertoire Coach and Session Musician.

Theo Clinkard (Movement Director)

Theo is dance artist and designer based in Brighton. He has performed with Siobhan Davies, Matthew Bourne's New Adventures, Wayne McGregor's, Random Dance, Lea Anderson, The Featherstonehaughs, Rafael Bonachela, Charles Linehan, New Art Club, Bgroup, Laila Diallo, Fin Walker, Mark Bruce and Volcano. In 2004, Theo co-founded PROBE with Antonia Grove. Together they commissioned, produced and performed new works from seven choreographers, including Yasmeen Godder's *i feel funny today* and *Accumulation* by Trisha Brown. Theo has worked on various commercial projects, including Kylie Minogue, for whom he choreographed the *Two Hearts* pop video and acted as assistant choreographer in the staging of her *Showgirl* and *Homecoming* tours. Theo's own creations include the dance film *(v) to leap or skip, especially in an emotional manner* with the filmmaker Mariko Montpetit, which screened at London's South Bank, and the solo work *P I L O T* for Brighton Fringe 2011. Forthcoming work includes a residency in Chile, where he will be leading master classes and creating new work for Cryptic, Glasgow to premiere in 2013. *Ten Plagues* continues Theo's on-going relationship with Stewart Laing, for whom he regularly designs costumes, including the forthcoming Traverse Theatre/Untitled Projects co-production, *The Salon Project*.

Zerlina Hughes (Lighting Design)

Zerlina graduated from Goldsmith's College in 1991 and holds an MA in Architectural Lighting. She has worked in theatre, opera, architectural lighting, television and film. Work for Opera includes: Bologna Opera, Malmö Opera, Norrlands Opera, Aix-en-Provence Festival, Théâtre des Champs Elysées, Reisopera (Netherlands); Scottish Opera, Almeida Opera, London Sinfonietta, Opera Northern Ireland, Covent Garden Festival, Cardboard Citizens and Grange Park Opera. Theatre work includes: National Theatre, Lyric Hammersmith, Glasgow Citizens Theatre, Stratford East, Nottingham Playhouse, Cheek by Jowl, and Actors Touring Company. Zerlina has also worked as assistant director to Mike Leigh.

Stewart Laing (Director and Designer)

Stewart Laing directs and designs theatre and opera. He is currently Artist in Residence at the Traverse. Work for the Traverse includes: *This is Water* and *An Argument about Sex* (co-produced with Untitled Projects and Tramway, Glasgow). Work for his Glasgow based company, Untitled Projects includes: *Blind Sight, Myths of the Near Future, Slope, The Drowned Giant.* and *The Salon Project*, which opens at the Traverse Theatre in October 2011. Stewart is a recipient of the 2010 Paul Hamlyn Breakthrough Fund to develop and expand Untitled Projects. Directing work for Opera includes Haydn's *La Fedeltà Premiata* (Bavarian State Opera); *Peter Grimes* (La Scala, Milan) and *La Boheme* (Scottish Opera). Stewart won a Tony Award for his design of *Titanic* on Broadway in 1997.

Conor Mitchell (Music)

Conor Mitchell is a musical dramatist. He trained with David Blake and Nicola LeFanu. He has written 13 music-plays including *The Dummy Tree* (National Theatre); *Gepetto in Spring* (Gotenberg, Sweden); *Diary of a Madman* (LAMDA, Drury Lane); *The Musician* (Cahoots NI); *The Rosen Street Protest* (NT Studio); *Merry Christmas Betty Ford* (Lyric Theatre); *Goblin Market* (NYMT) and *Pesach* (Waterfront Hall). He has written for the Ulster Youth Orchestra, twice been writer on attachment to the National Theatre, music adviser to YMT:UK and writer in residence at LAMDA. Awards include the Arts Foundation Fellowship Award for composition. Conor is working on the opera cycle *The Headless Soldier* with the playwright Mark Ravenhill - the first part of which premiered in London in August 2010 - as well as an oratorio for the London Gay Men's Chorus and a new opera in London. His music-play *The Doughboys* will premiere at the Belfast festival in 2012. He is 32 and lives in Northern Ireland.

Mark Ravenhill (Writer)

Mark previously worked with the Traverse in 2009 with *A Life in Three Acts*, co-written with Bette Bourne, subsequently performed at Royal Theatre in The Hague, Soho Theatre, London and St Ann's Warehouse New York, and in 2005 with *Product* (Paines Plough). Work for the National Theatre includes: *Nation, Citizenship , Education, Totally Over You and Mother Clap's Molly House,*. Work for the Royal Court includes: *Over There, Moscow* and *Shopping and Fucking* (co-produced with Out of Joint). Work for Terror includes: *The Experiment* and *Ripper*. Work for ATC includes: *Handbag* and *Faust is Dead*. Other work includes: *Ghost Story* (Playhouse); *Shoot/Get Treasure/ Repeat* (Paines Plough); *Pool - No Water* (Frantic Assembly, Lyric Hammersmith and Drum Theatre Plymouth); *Dick Whittington* (Barbican); *The Cut* (Donmar Warehouse); *North Greenwich* (Paines Plough); *Some Explicit Polaroids* (Out of Joint); *Handbag* (ATC); *Sleeping Around* (Salisbury Playhouse and Donmar Warehouse).

Finn Ross (Video Designer)

Finn Ross trained at Central School of Speech and Drama, London. He works across all forms of live performance with a particular interest in music, opera and devised work. Recent design work includes *Top Girls* (Chichester); *Rinaldo & Knight Crew* (Glyndebourne); *Simon Boccanegra, The Damnation of Faust & Don Giovanni* (English National Opera); *Free Run* (Udder Belly); *The Tell-Tale Heart & The Doctor's Tale* (Royal Opera House); *Greenland* (National Theatre); *Sunset Boulevard* (Gothenburg Opera); *Das Portrait* (Bregenz Opera Festival); *A Dog's Heart* (Dutch National Opera, English National Opera and Complicite); *The Gods Weep* (Royal Shakespeare Company); *MICroscop & Orlando* (Sadler's Wells); *Mr Brucek's Excursions to the Moon* and *15th Century Prague* (Opera North); *The Beggar's Opera* (Vanishing Point and Lyceum Edinburgh); *Serious Money* (Birmingham Rep); *The Girls of Slender Means* (Assembly Rooms); *Interiors* (Vanishing Point); *Shun-Kin* (Complicite at the Setagaya Public Theatre, Tokyo and Barbican, London); *All My Sons* on Broadway; *Little Otik* (Vanishing Point and National Theatre of Scotland); *Sugar Mummies* (Royal Court). *www.behance.net/ finnross*

SUPPORT THE TRAVERSE

Traverse Theatre – the Company

Contents

Introduction

The idea for writing a song cycle came from the composer Conor Mitchell. I got talking to Conor when he was working on a project of his own at the National Theatre studio and I was working on a project in another room. We discussed the possibilities of creating a piece of musical theatre together and quickly decided that we didn't want to write a conventional musical and that a full blown opera was an over ambitious start for a new collaboration. Conor suggested that a song cycle – an intense dramatic journey for a single voice and a piano – would be a good place for us to start working together. I didn't know very much about the classic song cycle so went away and got myself CDs and DVDs of Schubert's song cycles *Die Winterreise* and *Die schöne Müllerin*, still regarded as the greatest examples of the form. I became fascinated by the possibilities of working with such a restricted palette, of the interplay between a singer and a pianist, exploring the experience of a single protagonist.

Conor then suggested 'plague' as a subject. I went away and for many months read as much as I could about plague: the Biblical ten plagues, various histories of ancient and medieval plagues, Camus' existential writings. There was much that was fascinating but nothing that I felt any sort of personal connection with.

Then I found a paperback copy of Daniel Defoe's *A Journal of The Plague Year*. Like much of Defoe's writing, it passes itself as a factual document but is in fact an artfully constructed piece, drawing on documentary evidence from the London plague of 1665, mingled with Defoe's own childhood memories of the event and rounded off by a fair amount of the novelist's imaginings. Defoe's London, with its mercantile world and its population vacillating between godliness, superstition and pragmatic rationalism was a world that felt close enough to my own experience. During the year 1665 one third of the population of London died, one third fled and a third stayed and survived. My imagination was instantly engaged: I needed only to look out of my own window and wonder what would happen if one in three of my neighbours died within a year and whether I would be a victim, take flight or survive.

I also read Pepys' diaries. Pepys lived through the London plague but refers to it only infrequently in his diary. His tone is very different from Defoe's. Pepys is from the world of the court and the government, both of which Defoe is suspicious of, preferring to ally himself with merchants and workers. But there is a wry humanity in Pepys' writing that is thoroughly engaging and read alongside the Defoe it gave me a wider perspective on the events of 1665. Most of the imagery and incidents in my libretto for *Ten Plagues* are drawn either from Defoe or Pepys.

I was keen that Conor and I should write for a singer who could fully inhabit the intense emotion and black humour that our piece needed. I instantly thought of Marc Almond. For anybody of my generation, Marc is one of our most iconic pop stars. Since the 1980s, I'd watched with admiration as he had developed and broadened his repertoire to include all sorts of songs, including – particular favourites of mine – Kurt Weill and Jacques Brel. Both words and music for *Ten Plagues* were written with Marc in mind. When he joined us for a workshop on the piece at the Royal Court Theatre we could see that we were working with the perfect interpreter of the songs.

My work on *The Coronation of Poppea* came about when I met the team at Opera Up Close – Robin Norton-Hale, Ben Cooper and Adam Spreadbury Maher. I started to think about which operas might benefit from being performed in a small room behind a pub in north London. Opera today is nearly always performed in huge theatres and there's a real thrill in seeing a fantastic tenor filling a two thousand seat theatre with the full force of Verdi or Puccini. But Monteverdi was writing for a different, smaller venue and for a modestly sized band, with great emphasis on the words and vocal lines driving the drama. His operas *Orfeo* and *The Return of Ulysses* were written to be performed in rooms in front of an audience of courtiers while his *Coronation of Poppea*, written for one of the very first professional opera companies, was first performed in a theatre with the capacity of a modest sized West End playhouse.

The relationship between the gods and man are integral to *Orfeo* and *Ulysses* and, to a certain extent, *The Coronation of Poppea*. In a small room, I felt that we weren't best placed to realise gods, so I stripped them away from *Poppea*, alongside various other characters and incidents, losing almost half of Monteverdi's opera. This was not without huge regret as the whole piece is fantastic. But I was making a version for a particular space at a particular time, and a drama about eight human beings caught in a circle of obsession seemed to be the best strand to draw upon.

With *Ten Plagues* I wrote the words first and Conor wrote the music after. With *Poppea*, this was reversed. I had Monteverdi's score and then had to find new English words to fit the stresses and cadences of the original music. I was at the point of admitting defeat, overwhelmed by my own hubris as someone who neither speaks Italian or reads music. But I was encouraged and guided to continue with this challenge during a workshop with Alex Silverman and the singers Jessica Walker and Rebecca Caine. Without their timely intervention, I might have given up.

For me the combination of words and music to create a drama is an endlessly fascinating one. At the time of writing, I'm not sure what the future balance in my work will be between 'straight' plays and music theatre. But I'm sure these two libretti are just the beginning of a new adventure.

Mark Ravenhill
July 2011

Ten Plagues

a libretto

Songs

Spring

The spring is here

I'll buy
A ring
To wear
The spring is here

A door in Drury
Lane
Red cross
I want to buy a ring
The spring is here

A house shut up
The people say
May God preserve us
The spring is here

Above
A chamber
A woman's
Cry of grief

I want a ring
The spring is here

Bell tolls
Numbers called
The hearse of
Plague

The sun is out
I want a ring
The spring is here

Without a Word

Suddenly
I need a God

The pews are full
Each
Risking
Infection
To hear the Word

But
The pulpit is
Empty
The preacher fled

There is no Word

I want
To step up
Speak in tongues
Damn the preacher
Save us all

I leave
Without a word

Again to church

I want to preach
The King has fled
And courtiers
The palace empty
There is no rule

But I leave
Without a word

Church again
I want to preach
The merchant's gone
Great halls of grain and garments
All could steal and share
But I leave
Without a word

The surgeon
And physicians
Gone

No word

I hold my charm
I chant my spell

Abaracadabara
Abaracadabara
Abaracadabara

God grant the plague
Spares me
Alone

To Dream

Tonight
I went to see
The player say
To die
To die, to sleep
To sleep
Perchance to dream

Later
I dreamed
You pulled me down
And filled me
With your spittle
Sweat
And seed

If death is one long dream
Of you
Then send me plague
And let me die

But death is not a dream

Oh
Close the playhouse
Let the players starve
That I should think
That dead men dream

And
May your house be shut
A watchman placed
To keep you in
That made me wish for plague

I will not love you
I will not dream of you
I will not die

Market

Few go to market now
For fear of plague
But after weeks of
Bread
I must have meat
And so I go
To market

There's a pig
Hung up
That I
Desire

Opening my purse
I find the price

The butcher
Lays down a cup of vinegar
'Money here'
Butcher says
The butcher counts to ten
Before he takes the money out

And so I take my pig
Under my arm
Through empty streets

This is how business is done
When money is infection
In times of plague

The Pit

Some have no sign of plague
No token on body, face
They fall, no warning
On the street
Are gone

If I am visited
Let there be tokens on me
Let me blister
Swell and burn

And
If I should wake
To find
Swelling of my neck
Or groin
I shan't wait
For the carriers
And cart
To fetch me
Dead

But rather
I shall run
Through the streets

And
I shall reach the pit
Look down upon the hundred
Bodies
Tumbled there
And say

My friends
I'm here
I choose
To be with you
Hold me close in your
Embrace

And then I'll throw myself
Into the pit
Happy with
The company I keep

Farewell

You came
Into my room
Tonight
I almost
Kissed you but

You stopped me said
I've come to say goodbye

And still
I almost
Kissed you but

You stopped me said
I've found a tumour

And pulling up your shirt
Showed me
The token
Hard and round
A silver penny
Of contagion

This is my last day
You said
And so goodbye

I was frightened
That you'd kiss me

I could have hit you
For bringing your infection
Here

But I stood apart
And said
Goodbye

The time to kiss is over

No caress
Or bruise
Shall pass between us now
But stand apart
And leave you
To a house shut up
And cart
And pit

And so I neither hit you
Nor I kissed you
And you left

Goodbye

By Day

They say
Too many die
To carry them
At night
Into the pit
So by day
In brightest light
Plague corpses
Are brought
Through the city

I find
I must see
Just one
Body as it fell
The face
Of a man
As plague
Pulled him to death

I run about the city
Looking for the carts
And carriers
Now
Crowds fill the streets
To look on
Death

But
There is no display
No corpse to show

A guilty sadness

Growing dark and
Down an alley
By St Paul's
I see a body
A man who lay down
Of plague and died

I turn and run
I find
I don't want to see
A face at all

A New Law

A new law:
The healthy stay inside
From dusk
Let the infected walk
To take the air

What do you do
Parading the city
You almost dead?
Do you
Greet and pet each other thus

My sweet my dear
What tubors
See mine here
I die tomorrow
And you?
We'll have a pretty hearse

Or do you walk alone
Scared of one another
As we are scared of you?

Seeing You

The night was summer hot
And so I rose
And walked about
The city
No men
Fires
Burning
To purify the air

I came to
A place I'd never been
The pit

A man said:
Turn back
No place for you
This is the plague pit
You are clean

I don't know why
But I must go in
I said
Here's money
And he let me pass

None there
But carrier
Corpse
And me

The cart came soon
And tipping up
Spewed bodies
Out

How alike all were
Naked
Rotten
Each one
The same
Foul corpse

But then
As it fell
One face
Turned
And I saw
That it was you

You seemed to look at me
I felt your breath

I saw you yesterday
And now you're gone

Who once I loved
You're took

You seemed to look

But then the bodies
Ate you up

The earth was thrown
All covered
And I returned
And slept
Although
The night continued hot

The Wig

I've shaved myself
Removed
Each last hair
So that I am
Free
Of anything that may
House flea or lice

I've bought a wig
Had the barber set it just so
And in the mirror I
Admire myself
For hours

My neighbour says
There's infection
In that wig
The hair comes
From the heads of corpses
Tipped
Into the pits

I say
Wig, I'll burn you
In the morning
Lest you infect me
And all those I move amongst

But
Today
I put on my wig
And wear it
To the Exchange
Let it infect me
And all those I move amongst
In this dead man's hair
I'm beautiful

The Hermit

This September night
Three thousand died
Between the hours
Of one and three

When plague began
I should have fled
Found hedge or ditch
And lived alone
The only man

I could not
Flee
The city
Kept me

Three thousand dead
In just two hours

What
If all are took
But me?

What if all
The city
Fall about me
One by one?

What if I should bury
All
None left to
Bury me?

I shut the door
I will not move from here
Until the plague has passed

I wear my finest clothes
Alone

My ring
My wig
I feast and fast
Alone
I sit
Month after month

Dead to others
Alone
I live

But how like death
This solitude

Grief

When the plague first came
In spring
I heard the story of
A Lambeth mother
Whose daughter
Grew hot
And blistered
Died
That same night.
I shed tears
And everyone I told
Wept too

But now
In autumn
We see the bodies
In the street
The pits piled high
We go about our business
Our hearts still
Untroubled
All tears are gone

Now
I could see my friends
Family
Love
Fall into the grave
And I would not
Be moved

Now
If I die
Upon the street
All men would pass me
Too many gone
To mourn another

We all are plagued
Our hearts are gone
Our bodies live
We walking dead
About the city now

The Quaker

I knew him

His was a belief in quietness
Meetings of men
Who sit in silence
Listening to the Lord
Inside

He died
Of plague
Calmly
And was buried
Silently
As was his wish
Without a bell

I am not like him

If plague
Fetch me tonight
Let the bell
Be rung
That all the city knows
I am not a quiet man
But once was here
And now am lying in the pit

Keep ringing still
On on
Until the end of time
Tell men
Here was plague in London
And the dead are screaming still

Return

The numbers fall away
The worst is past
And so you're back
From Somerset

You tell me of the beauty of
Your rural life
How changed
The city is
You open up your shop
You start again

You say
You lived
I knew you would my friend

I drink with you
And smile
To see the city
Full again

You are foreign
To me now
You are a child of
Cruel innocence

You have not seen
What I have seen
Not known
The man fall dead
Beside you as you walked

I would not be you
I would not have your
Innocence
I'd rather see
What I have seen
Know
The city falling dead
Beside me as I walked

I come to your shop
Happily
But we'll never know each other
Now

Only those who live through plague
Can know each other
I do not know you

Ten Plagues

I am as an Israelite when
Ten plagues
Infect the land
I live

I see
The waters flow with blood
I live
Frogs outnumber men
I live
I see
Lice eat the people raw
I live
I could not see the sun
For flies
I live
Cattle fall and rot
I live
All about me blister
And I live
I see
Fire fall upon the earth
I live
Locusts swarm
I live
All is darkness
And I live

I watch
The angel
Pass over
The first-born die
Hear mothers
Maids
Sisters
Shout of grief
I live

I walk through
Parted waters
Turn and see
The merchant
Whore
Housewife
Doctor
All the city
Pulled into the sea
And gone
I live

Now
We never talk
Of plague
We live
We push our memory down
And live
Learn the new dance
Sing the new song
The shops fill
A new war
We live

Epilogue

In London
Came the plague in sixteen sixty-five
One hundred thousand dead
But I alive

The Coronation of Poppea

*freely adapted from the libretto by Giovanni Francesco Busenello
for* L'incoronazione di Poppea *by Claudio Monteverdi*

This version of *The Coronation of Poppea* opened at the King's Head Theatre, Islington, on 28 April 2011 with the following cast:

Liberto/Arnalta	Adam Kowalczyk
Nero	Jessica Walker
Poppea	Zoe Bonner
Ottavia	Rebecca Caine
Otto	David Sheppard
Drusilla	Jassy Husk
Seneca	Martin Nelson

Double Bass	Jonny Gee
Piano	Alex Silverman
Soprano saxophone	Chez Taylor

Directed by Mark Ravenhill
Musical direction/orchestration by Alex Silverman
Intervention aria composed by Michael Nyman
Designed by Katie Bellman
Lighting designed by William Reynolds

Characters

Liberto/Arnalta
Nero
Poppea
Ottavia
Otto
Drusilla
Seneca

Note: This libretto benefitted greatly from the suggestions of Alex Silverman and the cast of the first production. Michael Nyman suggested an additional scene (Scene Twenty-Two). To all of them I am hugely grateful.

Scene One

Liberto   What the fuck? What the fuck?
OK easy OK easy
No more no more dreams for Liberto
Get back to guarding Nero

Curse curse him him bloody Nero
Curse bloody Nero
Poppea
Fuck her and fuck Rome and this fucking
army

There's no rest no peace no sleep for the
people
When our Emp'ror's so corrupt
And the Emp'ress Ottavia fills dark night
with her weeping
While Nero makes Poppea his whore his
mistress
Seneca tries to warn him
But Nero doesn't give a toss
The Christians denounce him denounce him
denounce him
And he he just mocks them

And he and he
And he takes money from the people and
then gives it to the rich
We get all of the suffering
Meanwhile the crooks who rule over us grow
fat

Don't repeat don't repeat what I've said
tonight
Ev'ryone's an enemy
Your brother will kill you
And your mother hang you
When the times are as dark as those that we
endure

We who suffer we who suffer these dark
    times
We who suffer we who suffer these dark
    times
See each man must stand alone
We who suffer these dark times
See each man must stand alone

But dawn is now breaking
At last it's light
Here's Nero here's Nero
Here's Nero here's Nero
Quiet quiet
Nero is here

Scene Two

Poppea *and* **Nero**.

Poppea	My love my love please do not leave me
	My arms wrap round your neck like this so tight, so tightly
	Hold you just as your hands so beautiful
	Trap me hold me down
Nero	Poppea now I must leave you
Poppea	Oh don't go oh don't go my love oh do not leave me
	Daylight has barely broken
	And you who shine brightly here you're my sunlight
	Only you can warm like sunlight
	Without the light of love
	There's no point living
	Will you abandon me
	And leave and leave and leave and leave
	Me in darkness?
	Oh don't say that you'll go

Just one word this goodbye tastes so bitter
Oh my heart oh my soul see now how I die

Nero   We must do all we can to stop a scandal
We will tell the full story of our love
but only once we're sure Ottavia

Poppea   That she's what that she's what?

Nero   Sure that Ottavia's far from Rome in exile

Poppea   When will that be when will that be?

Nero   Sure that Ottavia's far from Rome in exile
When I've divorc'd her

Poppea   Go now go now oh hurry oh hurry
Go now go now oh hurry oh hurry
Go now oh hurry

Nero   Here on my lips my lips there comes
From deep within my heart
Here on my lips my lips there comes from
    deep within my heart
So many kisses my lover lover
But now goodbye
I promise you I will be back
I I promise you
I promise you I will be back oh my sweet
    goddess
I promise you I will be back oh my sweet
    goddess

Poppea   My love you see me always you see you see
You see me always but I
Don't believe always my love you see me
    always
You see you see you see me always
But I don't believe always because they say
That love is like a child who's blinded
And I know you will not you will not you will
    not

See how much I love your blind eyes
You will not you will not you will not see how
　　much I love
Your blind eyes

Nero　　I need your eyes to see so stay here with me
See so I stay here with you
Here forever Poppea treasure and light of
　　my world

Poppea　　Oh don't say that you'll go
Just one word this goodbye tastes so bitter
Oh my heart oh my soul see now how I die

Nero　　Have no fear have no fear
And stay with me stay with me here here
　　with me
In my arms
The light of my dark night
And proud goddess of my heart

Poppea　　You'll come back?

Nero　　Now I go away and yet I stay I stay right here

Poppea　　You'll come back?

Nero　　My body goes but still
But still my heart remains here with you

Poppea　　You'll come back?

Nero　　But I will not be long I will not I will not be
　　long be long
For that would be as fatal
As if I chopped off my hand and bled to
　　death
As if I chopped off my hand and bled to
　　death

Poppea　　You'll come back?

Nero　　I'll be back

Poppea	But when?
Nero	So soon love
Poppea	So soon love you promise soon love?
Nero	I'll be back
Poppea	You're sure you'll keep your word?
Nero	I'll be back in your bed or you'll be in mine
Poppea	You're sure you'll keep your word?
Nero	I'll be back in your bed or you'll be in mine
Poppea	Goodbye love
Nero	Goodbye love
Poppea	Oh Nero oh Nero goodbye love
Nero	Poppea Poppea goodbye love

Scene Three

Poppea   Still I wait to get the prize
So near not yet in my hand

Still I wait to get the prize
I'm greedy for my moment
In my mind I am already Emp'ress
But when I see my crown I'm dreaming
No no don't worry no no don't worry
No I can not fail

I am watch'd over watch'd over
Watched over by Love watched over by Love
And I am Fortune's child
The child of Fortune

Scene Four

Ottavia
Despised alone Ottavia Ottavia Ottavia
    despised alone
I am wife of an emp'ror
Abandoned abandoned abandoned woman
What now? What am I? What can I?

What a miserable sex is woman
We are awarded at our birth with the gift of
    freedom
But then marriage but then marriage
Locks all of us up and we're slaves
Our bodies spit out more men
Oh what a miserable sex is woman
At our breast we give suck to our own tyrant
We make milk and feed him up
So that he can flay us bleed us when he wants
By our own bodies we are doomd to make
    the very monster
Who will hurt us and then slowly kill us

My Nero my Nero my Nero my barb'rous
    Nero
My Nero my husband my husband
You bring me such great suffering in my life
And you curse me with this endless torment
Oh where are you? Oh where are you?

Lying with your Poppea lying with your
    Poppea with your Poppea
You're laughing you're happy
But while you're both happy laughing and
    loving
I am filling the night with bitter weeping
Do you lie beside her and do you laugh when
    you think of this sad woman?
Who once was proud but is now alone
Alone alone while you laugh

Oh fates above if there's a god
Listen to this my cry
Strike Nero down with lightning
Burn him up burn him up burn him up
    burn him up
Burn him with your flames

You are pointless
You're worthless
You're not worth the name of god
But no
Now I have said too much
And I am sorry
No more bitterness now no more
My suff'ring shall be silent

Scene Five

Poppea, Otto.

Poppea   Oh Otto please don't complain
                    Don't blame anyone but yourself if you can't
                        win
                    So you're unhappy about fate's fickle hand
                    But don't blame me for your luck
                    When dice are rolling up above us we have
                        no choice
                    The gods decide we
                    Mortals blindly do as we're told

Ottone   I knew when
                    I took you as my wife Poppea
                    That you felt nothing for me
                    But I hoped time would change your
                    Hard heart later I'd feel love
                    Grow in your breast
                    But now I see deep
                    Inside you all is coldness

You kill all all of my hope you kill all all of my
hope
And bury it deep

Poppea   Oh please no
Stop blaming me
Be a man man who suffers inside but stays
silent
Stop this stop this you think I'll come back
But my emperor tells me all that I must do
Your love means nothing your anger's
pointless
I'm leaving you so I can be so I can be
An emp'ress

Ottone   Oh I see oh I see now that nothing
Nothing matters more to you than power

Poppea   I see I see that you are nothing
Pathetic fool you are clinging to nothing all
gone

Ottone   I gave you all my love
And this is my reward?

Poppea   Enough just stop

Ottone   I gave you all my love
And this is my reward?

Poppea   Just stop just stop goodbye I'm Nero's

Scene Six

Otto   Otto Otto wake wake up to the cold truth
She might be beautiful when you look at the
outside
But she has nothing else she is not human
Wake up wake up my heart wake up to the
truth
So she says she'll be Emp'ress

And if she succeeds when she succeeds
Then she won't want you still breathing
Otto wake up wake to the cold truth
You'll be a reproach when she lies with her
    Nero
She won't want you still living
So she'll start something a cruel plan to kill
    you
Power buys someone
Who will bring false accusations
That I'm disloyal that I'm a traitor
Once they've started my ruin with their false
    words
Then nothing will stop innocence
Being slaughtered

No she must be stopped
I'll take up a weapon a weapon or give her
    poison
Someone must destroy her yes
Someone must destroy her she is vermin

So this is this's what becomes of our
Love here's where it all ends
My love all ends
With your foul betraying heart
Foul betraying heart Poppea

Scene Seven

Ottone, Drusilla.

Drusilla	Still ev'rything is Poppea You only talk of you're always calling her name
Otto	She's not here in my heart only in my mouth So that from my spit the wind will quickly carry

	The name of that foul woman who betrayed me
	And turned my love to hatred
Drusilla	Up in the court of Love justice is being done
	So you must show mercy
	To this poor woman whose thoughts are all of you
Otto	I'll give myself to you oh wonderful woman
	Ev'rything I have is now yours
	I don't want don't want anyone else
	There's just you just you for me
	Drusilla my love oh please
	Forgive all the foolish things that I've done
	I know I've hurt you
Drusilla	Can you forget
	So quickly the one who once you loved
	Otto do you do you Otto
	Finally have a heart to share with me?
Otto	It's here Drusilla Drusilla here yes yes
Drusilla	You say say these words
	Are they real or are you lying?
Otto	No no Drusilla Drusilla no
Drusilla	Otto these words
	Otto these words just words just words
Otto	I only speak the truth looking at you
Drusilla	But love
Otto	I need you
Drusilla	But is this love?
Otto	I need you I need you
Drusilla	So suddenly like that?
Otto	My love's a fire
	So suddenly burning

Drusilla These hasty words of passion
Feel good feel good
Reaching my heart reaching
Reaching I feel good my heart
But you don't mean this
Is this real love?

Otto I need you I need you
I think only of you and your beauty
There's a sharp new picture branded in my
    heart here
And it's you beautiful you it's you beautiful
You must believe it's true

Drusilla I must go now smiling smiling smiling
I must go Otto I must go smiling
I'll make you happy I'll make I'll make you
    will be happy
I must hurry to our poor unhappy Em'press

Otto The tempest of my heart the tempest of my
    heart
Finally falls calm
She is mine for ever she is mine for ever my
    Drusilla
I wish I could feel love for her
Now Drusilla is on my lips
But Poppea Poppea is in my heart still

Scene Eight

Nero, Seneca.

Nero I've done it I've made up my mind
Seneca my wise teacher
Today I will divorce my wife
And I'll put my new wife upon the throne
Upon the throne upon the throne
Poppea

Seneca	My lord When feelings are a guide to action Then we may live to regret it Never trust to passion When you have a choice to make better judgement Trust reason's power not passion
Nero	For me reason is Too rigid a dogma It's fit for weak men But it's not for an emp'ror
Seneca	Not so men will obey more readily when they see Logical logical rulers upon the throne
Nero	Don't give me lectures I want her if I want want her then I'll have her
Seneca	You will provoke you will provoke you will provoke the people And the senate
Nero	Damn the senate And the people too I don't care
Seneca	Then take care of yourself And your reputation
Nero	I'll cut out the tongue Of any man who speaks out
Seneca	When one man's tongue is stopped Then more will speak out
Nero	Octavia is getting old Her body's barren
Seneca	This is an excuse It's not the real cause

Nero	My law is the law my law is the law is Whatever I choose
Seneca	The law is the law is Greater than your word
Nero	All men must follow my word
Seneca	There will be blood shed There'll be blood shed
Nero	I've got no time for Your logical reason
Seneca	Laws of reason laws of Reason must rule over earth and Heaven

Nero	You you you are provoking my anger
	Provoking anger
	Make me angry make me angry make me
	    angry make me angry
	I don't hear you and all the people
	And the senate and Octavia and the gods
	    and all
	Hell fire won't stop me
	If it's right or it's wrong
	Right or it's wrong I will do this marry marry
	I'll do it today I'll do it
	Today I'll do it today
	I'll have her

Seneca	I have lost him now he will Always always always go his own way What can we do when tyrants Ignore all reason?

Scene Nine

Nero, **Poppea** *and* **Liberto**.

Poppea	Tell me sweetest lover tell me how lov'ly
	Remember the perfection that night without end
	When from these sweet lips came kisses
Nero	You bit me bit me you bit me bit me and it was wonderful
Poppea	And how was and how was the touch of my my my breast
Nero	No words can describe it can describe no words describe
	How good was the touch of your breast of your breast how good
Poppea	These lover's these lover's strong lover's strong arms
	Which held me held held me all night long
Nero	I want you always here in my arms in my arms
	Always in my arms always to have you to have you
	Poppea my breathing's stopping
	I look at your lips
	Remember how with kisses
	They could fire me they could inflame me
	With hot passions
	Oh oh lover lover they could arouse me
	No more more in the heavens lies my fate
	But in these sweet lips now but in these sweet lips now
	But in these sweet lips here
	Of wonderful red

Poppea   My love my love you give me these words
which so sweet
Are here in my soul my being
I repeat them over again
And these words which move inside
Without end will melt at once this lover's
sweet heart
Oh these your fine words I hear them
Oh your kisses kisses I taste them
The sound of your voice of your voice so
good
It thrills me so completely so and so totally
That not content with not content with not
content with filling up my head
It pierces through my breast my heart my
heart it kisses
That not content with not content with not
content with filling up my head
It pierces through my breast my heart my
heart it pierces

Nero   This imperial crown I wear means I rule
over
The multitude decide the fates of half the
world
With you with you I want to share this
And so I'll only be happy
When you are standing beside me as my
em'press

What what are these words these words oh
Poppea
How tiny is Rome for your majesty
For your greatness all Italy is no match
With your great beauty it must be an insult
To ask you to be Emp'ror Nero's bride

And the only thing that's wrong with your
fair eyes wrong with your fair eyes

They're not for humans they're far above
    nature
But with modesty they don't compete with
    heaven
All I can offer you is this poor praise
I'm silenced by your beauty I can only stare

Poppea   The highest hope I know is now beating here
Because you say I am yours
My reputation's safe because you want me
But there are far too many things to hold us
    back
Even emp'ror's promises can be empty
    words
Seneca is your master
At his wise Stoic gatherings
That cunning philosopher
Is always telling the people gathered there
He's the power he's the power behind the
    Emperor's throne

Nero   Him? Him?

Poppea   That he's the power his power's behind the
    Emperor's throne

Nero   That decrepit old man

Poppea   Him him

Nero   Has dared to say this?

Poppea   Has dared to say this

Nero   Hey you go now Liberto
To Seneca's gathering and say these words to
    him
You are commanded to kill yourself
And remember this the power is mine alone
No philosopher or his Stoic words can stop
    me
To think that I could ever

Have suppressed my strong spirit put my
    faith
In following the crass teachings
Of philosophy I know far more than him
Poppea Poppea oh show me your smile oh
    oh show me your smile
Today we'll show the world love always wins
We'll show the world love always wins

Scene Ten

Liberto, **Seneca**.

Liberto

When a tyrant gives orders
There isn't any reason
And it will always end with violence
And murder
So I am the killer
Although I'm doing nothing but following
    orders
My conscience really should not be so
    troubled
The victim's blood falls on my hands
Seneca Seneca if I had a choice
I would leave now
I was told I was sent here
Please don't blame me for this
Don't look in my eyes
But I must do I must do
The very last thing I want to

Seneca

Liberto
I've been waiting to hear this for a long time
Knowing this would be my fate
When you live in such dark times then you
    know
That your end will come quickly
At any moment

If you tell me I must die
I will listen and not blame
Come smile
When you give me this gift that you bring

Liberto   Nero has

Seneca   I know I know

Liberto   Commanded me to

Seneca   I understand you
And I will follow orders

Liberto   You understand all this when I can't say it?

Seneca   As soon as I saw you
That's when I knew it was him who sent you
That's when I knew exactly what news you
     would tell me
And that you brought me orders
That I must be ready to die
Great Nero has sent you to me with this
     command
To kill myself

Liberto   Yes sir that is what he told me
May death may death grant you peace
May death grant you peace
Knowing that just as we count the days
By looking to the sky to see the sun
So shall all future people think and write
     using
The light of your philosophy
May death may death grant you peace
May death grant you peace

Seneca   Leave now leave now leave me now go back
If you see Nero before nightfall say it's done
I'm dead and I'm buried
You have done well

Scene Eleven

Seneca   Alone for a final moment
In the mind all is peaceful
There is safety within me
This world's only what I see
In my soul I can make all of this earthly
        beauty
Leaving behind the ugly world of struggle
Ah yes all is peace within
Freely freely I'll leave now
No more aching for fame for wealth
All the struggles that steal peace from my
        soul
Here I am still as the water and water will
        take me
All is done
I am ready

Come my friends come my friends
Time has come time has come
To put into practice what I've taught you
As a theory for a long time
Death's nothing a moment's pain
Then at last the breath
Escapes this weak body
Where for so many years it's held as a
        pris'ner
Without light or freedom
Now it can fly to Olympus
To freedom and to live in true happiness

Followers   No don't die no don't die no
You shouldn't choose to die
Not when life is full of goodness
Not when daylight comes each morning
All our pain all our suffering
Is nothing but an illusion
Is nothing but an illusion

It is good to let sleep claim you
But then wake again when it's morning
From a tomb of heavy marble
You will never see a new day
No don't die

Seneca

See now my companions
With what great ease I do this
For life goes on regardless like a river
    before us
So may this warm flow of blood
With the force of a river
Carry me carry me away as blood flows
As I watch as I watch
My life pass

Scene Twelve

Seneca

Seneca said:
My friend I cannot stop your tears
But I can wipe your eyes
Yes death has taken me from you
Don't grieve for long
Yes you have left your homeland
Don't look back
To cry for ever is indulgence
To never shed a tear never shed a tear
Is not human
We are human
We have both head and heart
We feel longing
Which we conquer

Scene Thirteen

Ottavia, Otto.

Ottavia	You who my family bestowed the title you now bear If you feel any gratitude then you must listen And do as I ask do as I ask do as I ask
Otto	When an em'press commands I will do whatever is asked Tell me what tell me what I must do For you you my Emp'ress I'll do anything you ask of me Even if it means I give up my life
Ottavia	I want I want I want you to take this weapon And turn this dull blade red with the blood of the blood of Poppea Go now and kill her go now and kill her Go now and kill her
Otto	Who must I kill? Who must I kill? Who?
Ottavia	Poppea
Otto	Kill who you say? Kill who you say? Who must I kill?
Ottavia	Poppea
Otto	Poppea? Poppea? I must murder Poppea?
Ottavia	Poppea Poppea what's this Were they just empty words when you made your promise?
Otto	What did I promise? What did I promise? These were just words of custom without thinking The polite words of a subject flatt'ring a queen Will you condemn me will you condemn me To a traitor's death?

Ottavia   What are these words? What are these feeble
               words?

Otto   I'm asking I'm asking whoever listens up
               above
               Give me the strength for this hard task

Ottavia   Better to kill her now waiting won't help you
               The quicker you do this
               The sooner it is over

Otto   Is it today when I must die?
               Is today when I must die?

Ottavia   Are you still standing there talking to
               yourself?
               Oh I warn you oh I warn you
               If you will not now obey my imperial
               command
               Then you will pay a great cost a great cost for
               your
               Slowness will cost your life

Otto   But if she knows it's me?

Ottavia   Hide in hide in a disguise
               Dress yourself in the clothes of some poor
               woman
               Make sure no one will know you
               Use ev'ry art and trick there is
               But just be sure that it's done

Otto   Oh how quickly how quickly must I teach
               these shaking
               Hands to stab her
               Must I so quickly calm my beating heart that
               once
               Loved her?
               Oh now I'll fill it with nothing but the still
               coldness
               Of a killer

Ottavia   You must do this right now
If you don't do this right now then I will
 accuse I will accuse you
Of attempted rape against my royal person
Then you will be taken from here and locked
 up in chains
You'll be tortured you'll be tortured
Then sentenced you'll have a slow death

Otto   Then I must obey my Em'press' commands
It is done
You gods you gods oh you gods
Strike me down please kill me
I'd rather die than do this terrible murder

Scene Fourteen

Otto, Drusilla.

Drusilla   Are you leaving
Leaving me love?

Otto   Drusilla Drusilla

Drusilla   Leaving leaving me your lover?

Otto   I'm looking I'm looking
I'm looking for you

Drusilla   Here I am here I am
And I am yours

Otto   Drusilla I have something a secret
Something so terrible so terrible you
Must promise you will keep this to yourself

Drusilla   My self I give to you
And all I own is yours to take from me
Take whatever you want is all yours
I'm listening I'm listening
Please tell me

I will keep secret whatever you want you can
   tell me
I'm on your side

Otto
You must forget your envy yes
You must forget your envy of Poppea

Drusilla
No no

Otto
Of Poppea

Drusilla
Here my heart fills
With such happiness I'm so happy
Here as my heart swells

Otto
Listen listen
I must without delay
Carry out my orders which are that
When I find her I must kill her
So she does not know I'm the one who kills
   her so coldly
I must do it in your dress

Drusilla
Take my dress
Everything I have take it my love

Otto
I I can kill without trace
Then you and I can live together
Living a life of nothing but love
If I die for this murder
Then cry for me as I am buried
Speak nothing but kind words
Oh speak kind words
Oh oh Drusilla
And if I run far away if I run far away to
   escape
From Nero far from Nero's cruel
   punishment
Then help me then help me to escape

Drusilla
Take my dress ev'rything I have take it
Love I will give you

I will give you anything anything
Anything I will give you
You must take great care
Love do this with great care
Whatever happens
Whatever happens believe me
That my life is lived only for you
I am worth nothing
All I live for is to please you
I'll show you now Drusilla's love is a greater
   love
Than any other
No love as great as great as my love
Come on let's do this
I am filled with your love
My heart beats like a drum
My heart beats like a drum
My heart beats like a drum
Come let's do this
Take my dress now
You must wear this
Must wear this must wear this
When you kill her in disguise
But I must know
What has driven you my love to commit such
   a murder
You must tell me

Otto   Let's go
It's time to do it
And I'll tell you ev'rything
You will be amazed

Scene Fifteen

Poppea, Arnalta.

Poppea   Now that Seneca's dead meat
Cupid Cupid Cupid listen to me

Make me make me what I long to be
A married woman married woman
Married woman married woman
With a crown
Cupid Cupid Cupid Cupid
Listen to me
Make me make me what I long to be
A married woman a married woman a
    married woman

Now I feel like I must sleep
I will shut my eyes
And take a moment's slumber
Here on the ground Arnalta I'll make my
    bed
And at one with nature
I'll sleep just as you see me
Soothed by the breeze on my brow

But if my sleep is far too deep
I shall sleep far too long
Then you must come and wake me
And don't allow a single person to come here
Drusilla can come
She is my only true friend

Arnalta   Rest yourself now Poppea
Let yourself sleep now my sweet mistress
You are watched over by me
Oblivion will take you
With his gentle caresses
He soothes you til you slumber
Don't let me see your eyes op'ning
Keep them closed
And let sleep claim you
Give yourself over to silence
Poppea now you are sleeping
Rest has come to take you and give you sweet
    dreams

Sleep now dear oh
Sleep now oh
Sleep now my dear oh sleep

Scene Sixteen

Otto *in a dress,* **Poppea**, **Arnalta**.

Otto   Here I am here I am
I was a man but now I'm Drusilla
Now I'm Drusilla no man
I am now Drusilla no no man
I am now Drusilla

I am a serpent
I carry here a poison
More deadly than any snake before me

Oh have I missed my chance here?
No she sleeps so sleep my heart
Your eyes are shut now
But will they stay like this?
It's best that you sleep
Best not see what I must do
You'll never see this strange woman
Who comes here as your killer
This woman must now hold you
And never let go

What's this? Trembling and tearful
What's this? What's this?
I am far too weak
What's this? My heart stops in my weak chest
My stomach's aching
Such a blinding pain here
What are my eyes blinded by the light now?
I'm crying such tears oh
What if this deed is not for a woman
But needs a man's cruelty?

What so troubled so troubled?
She hasn't ever loved me
Do I still love her?
I gave my promise I'd do this
If I should fail then I know
That I'll be the one who will be facing death's
     sting

There's no place at court
For a man who is good
Only those men who look after their own
     needs do well
The rest are blind fools
No one will see me kill her
And in time the mem'ry
Of this will be buried inside
Poppea Poppea here comes death
My love my hope all die here die

The spirit of Amore possesses **Otto***:*

You're a dead man you're a killer
An enemy of all good men
Who do you think who do who do you think
     you are
You're the one who should take the knife
No you're not fit to be killed by the same
     knife
That's meant for your love run away
You will not die by this
But you will be hunted down and then
The hangman will end your sad life

Poppea   Drusilla Drusilla
Why was she here
And why was this knife in her hand
As I lay here sleeping in my garden?

Arnalta   Come help here come help here
Ev'ry one of you must help us in the search
     to find her

Find Drusilla find her Drusilla Drusilla
Hurry hurry hurry
Such a creature must be found
She must not get away
Find Drusilla
Hurry hurry hurry

Scene Seventeen

Drusilla

I am dreaming I'm dreaming
Drusilla you are dreaming
Can this be real?
Longing all my lifetime all my lifetime
All my lifetime, all my lifetime long
And now here it's coming
Now's the time she must die she must die
Now's the time now's the time now's the time
She must die the bitch will die soon
And Otto will love me
And Otto will love me at last
He'll be he'll be he'll be he'll be he'll be my
    love
I am dreaming I'm dreaming
Drusilla you are dreaming
Can this be real?
He wears my dress as he twists the knife in
    her
As she looks up she calls out too late
You gods who rule above us
I tell you I must wear I tell you I must wear
That blood-stained dress
Oh I am dreaming I'm dreaming
Drusilla you are dreaming
Can this be real?

Scene Eighteen

Arnalta, **Nero**, **Drusilla**.

Arnalta	My lord here she is the witch
	Who attempted to stab my poor mistress
	Poppea
	Who lay peaceful as a lamb
	In her beautiful garden
	But then came this vile woman drew
	A knife a knife to kill her
	If I had not then woken up
	And instantly saved her
	From that cold blade from that cold blade
	She would now be slaughtered
Nero	How could you even think this?
	And who is the mur'drous traitor
	Who made you do this?
Drusilla	I am totally
	Blameless I
	Have a clear free conscience
	I did not do this
Nero	You must
	Confess must confess confess to your crime
	You were driven by hatred
	Or you were ordered to commit
	Murder or you were paid
	A hired killer
Drusilla	I am totally
	Blameless I
	Have a clear free conscience
	I did not do this
Nero	Whip her hard whip her hard
	Locked up locked up
	Torture torture
	Until you break down

Until you are begging
To name that traitor
I want names I want names
I want names all their
Names of ev'ry single
Traitor

Drusilla   Curse you cruel gods if
Nero has me tortured then
I know that I'd break and I'd
Tell tell the one name I
Hold close
So I must say yes I'm the one who did this it's
Me and so they must hang me
Oh oh
You who say you live by
True love's virtue
Look what this woman
Does and tell me was there
Ever love like
My love?

Arnalta   What's that chatt'ring murd'ress?

Nero   What words are these you traitor?

Drusilla   Such torment here in
My head a pain here
Tears me apart here's love
But here's innocence

Nero   Quick before I'm too
Angry then
I will give the word
And you'll be tortured
Give up this
Stubborn silence and tell me
Ev'ry single last word of
Your demented plotting

Drusilla   My lord
What she is saying

                      Is true it
                      Was me I tried
                      To kill Poppea

Nero   Take this woman take this woman from
                      Here and have her cruelly
                      Tortured
                      Tell them I want her dead but slowly
                      Let her feel life slowly
                      Seeping from her as she is
                      Broken by the torturers'
                      Weapons dragging
                      Her pain-rack'd body towards a hard death

Drusilla   Oh my love oh my one love
                      You must never
                      Forget weep bitter
                      Tears as I hang
                      Just this once
                      Say you'll cry I know you'll
                      Never be in love with me but maybe you
                          could still shed
                      Tears because I love
                      You
                      I go now they will
                      Torture and kill me
                      But I will always love you
                      Even as they hang me I'll
                      Love you I'll so
                      Be proud I died
                      For your crime

Scene Nineteen

Otto, Nero, Drusilla.

Otto   Wait wait wait
                      She is not the one don't punish her
                      I am the one I must be punished

Drusilla   Kill me kill me take my
                   Life it was me who came knife in hand to kill
                      Poppea

Otto   By all the gods in
                   Heaven above
                   She's innocent she didn't do
                   This

Drusilla   No one did this but
                   This hand and this heart so full
                   With hate hate drove me
                   Hate lying deep in this foul
                   Body don't waste
                   More time take me and
                   Execute me

Otto   She's innocent she didn't
                   Do this
                   Kill me
                   Kill me this is
                   Drusilla's own dress I wore
                   This dress by
                   Order of the Empress our queen Ottavia
                      who gave this
                   Knife to murder sweet Poppea kill me
                   Kill me my lord
                   Come take the knife and
                   Kill me

Drusilla   Kill me you must kill
                   Me I'm the one who took this traitor's
                   Knife to Poppea

Otto   Come Heaven and show
                   Your rage throw your fires upon
                   Me here I want pain just as great
                   As this my crime I want to die I
                   Must be punished

Drusilla   I must be punished

Otto   I must be punished

Drusilla Kill me

Otto   Kill me

Drusilla Kill me

Otto   I must be punished
Kill me my
Lord come take this
Knife and kill
Me but maybe
You can't but maybe I'm not
Worthy of the time spent
In killing
I know that I am far too lowly
To kill and you would rather
I lived with this
Torment
You could order my
Torture hear me as
Screaming I am whipped for
My crimes or you
Could make the lions feed on
My flesh let them swallow up
All my guilty conscience
Or you could leave alive
Endlessly in
Torment

Nero   Live live but
Go leave here in
Exile to wander through
All the hostile world always a
Pauper and
Lost alone you'll beg for scraps to
Feed on when you rest in some
Dark cave you'll dream of
Your crime

And you
Who offered up your
Life you most worthy
Woman so you could save the
Life of this most unworthy man whose love
   you
Live for
Live so all see how Nero
Sometimes forgives
Live so all see what a good
Woman looks like
Let all men in Rome be
Told how steadfast
You are may ev'ry woman
May ev'ry woman
Be as trustworthy as you

Drusilla   Let me go with him
Let me go
With him into exile
Only with him am I
Happy I'm happy I'm
Happy

Nero   Go then
You want him have him

Otto   My lord my lord not punished
At all not punished at all
Not punished at all
She is my
Reward she is my
Reward she
Is my reward
This woman is all I need she is my
Wealth and my fame
Are here
With me

Drusilla   To live by your side
And to die with you is all

I want
Family money are nothing now
I have all I need
Family money are nothing now
I have all I need you're with
Me and now
You see that here in
My heart I will be
Faithful always

Nero   Here is my
Most solemn judgement
This is what I now
Command I here divorce
Ottavia take
Her and let her be sent far
Far away
Never to return
Go now Ottavia and look out
Across the sea
There's a boat waiting to take you
Ready to speed you away you will be
Carried wherever the sea and the winds are
Blowing
Ev'rything is now
Settled I am happy
Poppea is now my queen

Scene Twenty

Ottavia   No no no I will not cry
I I I leave my homeland
Leave leave my friends my friends
Say goodbye
I am innocent but I must leave today
When I'm far away then maybe tears will
     find me

When I'm wand'ring distant lands and lost
    all hope
Then I might weep

My home
Always I I thought that this was home
But no more
There is no home for me
And I must wander all the world
If I speak or dream of Rome then
I'll shut my mouth close my eyes tight
Until I can forget that once
There was Rome
Inside me must be nothing
No Rome no homeland

There's an ocean there's a wide sea
A wide sea that will carry me far from here
From all that I am
From all that I am
Far far far from myself
From Rome

No no no I must never allow one tear
I must forget who I am
I will never look back towards Rome

Heart's empty
My soul is all dullness
I'm finished with hurt
Nothing more in my dead heart
As I leave you
There's pain no more
Longing for my home

Nothing more in my dead heart
I leave you
No pain
No more longing for my home
I am gone

Scene Twenty-One

Arnalta   Good girl good girl
Today Poppea today Poppea
Will be crowned will be crowned as our
    Em'press
Me too her faithful old nurse
I'm promoted upwards with my girl
New heights
No more commoners no more commoners
No commoners no common talk with low
    commoners
People once once said 'You'
Now will show me more respect
They'll bow low to me
'Good day to you my lady good day to you
    lady'
If I see them in town they'll stop to say
'You look fabulous what skin
So young so young such ageless beauty
You are ageless'
I'll say 'Yes'
Even though I know that I'm almost forty
Well really over forty
I'll allow them all of the flatt'ry
When really I know they're users
Just looking for a good word to Poppea from
    me
They'll need me
I'll drink deep from the full cup of flatt'ry
I'll drink up ev'ry last drop
Ev'ry last drop of that cup of lies
Born as a servant
I will die on I will die on I'll die on the A list
I don't want to die
Give me my time once more
Give me my time once more
Give me my time once more
I'd be born as a lady I'd die a servant

If you end your life at the top
Death comes and it takes from you
But how sweet is how sweet is death's kiss
When your life's been hard work
Death brings you peace at last

Scene Twenty-Two

Ottavia   In exile
Ottavia knew
(Says Tacitus)

Ottavia knew
(Says Tacitus)
That death would come

Oh cut my veins
I will not bleed
A scalding bath
I will not bleed
At last the rope
I suffocate

A knife they cut
(Says Tacitus)
My head away

So Poppea
(Says Tacitus)
Could see it cold

She looks at me
I look at her
I pity her
The dead can read
Says Tacitus
Poppea's fate

Soon Poppea's
Womb grew a boy
But Nero kicked

Poppea bled
(Says Tacitus)
And lost the boy

She looks at me
And I look back
No pity no
The dead can read
Says Tacitus
Poppea's fate

Poppea died
The people wept
To see her pass

A public show
But in their hearts
They hated her

Oh cut my veins
I will not bleed
A scalding bath
I will not bleed
The rope won't hurt
I will not die

Scene Twenty-Three

Nero/Poppea   When I see you
When I touch you
When I kiss you
When I hold you
No more aching
No more crying
No more dying
When you still me
With pleasure fill me full
I am yours
You are mine

We are one
Always one
You're my life
We are gods
And it's good
Yes so good
When I see you
When I touch you
When I kiss you
When I hold you
No more aching
No more crying
No more dying
When you still me
With pleasure fill me full

Methuen Drama Student Editions

Jean Anouilh *Antigone* • John Arden *Serjeant Musgrave's Dance*
Alan Ayckbourn *Confusions* • Aphra Behn *The Rover* • Edward Bond
Lear • *Saved* • Bertolt Brecht *The Caucasian Chalk Circle* • *Fear and
Misery in the Third Reich* • *The Good Person of Szechwan* • *Life of Galileo* •
Mother Courage and her Children • *The Resistible Rise of Arturo Ui* • *The
Threepenny Opera* • Anton Chekhov *The Cherry Orchard* • *The Seagull* •
Three Sisters • *Uncle Vanya* • Caryl Churchill *Serious Money* • *Top Girls*
• Shelagh Delaney *A Taste of Honey* • Euripides *Elektra* • *Medea* •
Dario Fo *Accidental Death of an Anarchist* • Michael Frayn *Copenhagen*
• John Galsworthy *Strife* • Nikolai Gogol *The Government Inspector* •
Robert Holman *Across Oka* • Henrik Ibsen *A Doll's House* • *Ghosts* •
Hedda Gabler • Charlotte Keatley *My Mother Said I Never Should* •
Bernard Kops *Dreams of Anne Frank* • Federico García Lorca *Blood
Wedding* • *Doña Rosita the Spinster* (bilingual edition) • *The House of
Bernarda Alba* • (bilingual edition) • *Yerma* (bilingual edition) • David
Mamet *Glengarry Glen Ross* • *Oleanna* • Patrick Marber *Closer* • John
Marston *Malcontent* • Martin McDonagh *The Lieutenant of Inishmore* •
Joe Orton *Loot* • Luigi Pirandello *Six Characters in Search of an Author*
• Mark Ravenhill *Shopping and F***ing* • Willy Russell *Blood Brothers*
• *Educating Rita* • Sophocles *Antigone* • *Oedipus the King* • Wole
Soyinka *Death and the King's Horseman* • Shelagh Stephenson *The
Memory of Water* • August Strindberg *Miss Julie* • J. M. Synge *The
Playboy of the Western World* • Theatre Workshop *Oh What a Lovely
War* Timberlake Wertenbaker *Our Country's Good* • Arnold Wesker
The Merchant • Oscar Wilde *The Importance of Being Earnest* •
Tennessee Williams *A Streetcar Named Desire* • *The Glass Menagerie*

Methuen Drama Modern Plays

include work by

Edward Albee
Jean Anouilh
John Arden
Margaretta D'Arcy
Peter Barnes
Sebastian Barry
Brendan Behan
Dermot Bolger
Edward Bond
Bertolt Brecht
Howard Brenton
Anthony Burgess
Simon Burke
Jim Cartwright
Caryl Churchill
Complicite
Noël Coward
Lucinda Coxon
Sarah Daniels
Nick Darke
Nick Dear
Shelagh Delaney
David Edgar
David Eldridge
Dario Fo
Michael Frayn
John Godber
Paul Godfrey
David Greig
John Guare
Peter Handke
David Harrower
Jonathan Harvey
Iain Heggie
Declan Hughes
Terry Johnson
Sarah Kane
Charlotte Keatley
Barrie Keeffe

Howard Korder
Robert Lepage
Doug Lucie
Martin McDonagh
John McGrath
Terrence McNally
David Mamet
Patrick Marber
Arthur Miller
Mtwa, Ngema & Simon
Tom Murphy
Phyllis Nagy
Peter Nichols
Sean O'Brien
Joseph O'Connor
Joe Orton
Louise Page
Joe Penhall
Luigi Pirandello
Stephen Poliakoff
Franca Rame
Mark Ravenhill
Philip Ridley
Reginald Rose
Willy Russell
Jean-Paul Sartre
Sam Shepard
Wole Soyinka
Simon Stephens
Shelagh Stephenson
Peter Straughan
C. P. Taylor
Theatre Workshop
Sue Townsend
Judy Upton
Timberlake Wertenbaker
Roy Williams
Snoo Wilson
Victoria Wood

For a complete catalogue
of Methuen Drama titles
write to:

Methuen Drama
Bloomsbury Publishing Plc
36 Soho Square
London W1D 3QY

or you can visit our website at:

www.methuendrama.com